AF580472

ENDING A RELATIONSHIP

MOVING ON AFTER A BREAKUP

SOPHIA KIMMONS

Copyright © 2022 Sophia Kimmons
All rights reserved.
ISBN: 9798848718270

ENDING A RELATIONSHIP: MORNING ON AFTER ENDING A RELATIONSHIP

TABLE OF CONTENTS

CHAPTER 7: BENEFITS

CHAPTER 8: MOVING ON

CONCLUSION

INTRODUCTION

Do you wish to divorce your spouse or end your romantic relationship? If so, you must be aware of the manner in which to end a relationship . Unbelievable as it may seem, there are guidelines for ending a relationship.

It's crucial that you proceed cautiously if you've been dating your partner for a while. You cannot simply text them to inform them that the event is over. In fact, if you've been dating someone for between two and five years, this is the worst way to break up. Typically, if you've been dating someone for this long, it's likely they have strong feelings for you. Keep in mind that over the years, you both have created priceless memories of each other, so even if you feel ready to move on, they might not.

You must explain it to them gradually for precisely this reason. They can be unaware that the relationship has a problem. Some people experience intense feelings after a breakup, including anxiety, depression, and even anger. Always be mindful of other people's feelings and avoid playing with them. Always break up in person, and if you want to avoid any drama, do it where there are many people around. You're not sure if your lover will sob or yell. If your relationship with them is strong, you won't be able to spare them from being hurt. People are often quite delicate. We won't be able to reproduce or continue living without a partner. This is not to argue that there aren't contented single individuals in the world.

Find out your reasons for wanting to end the relationship now, before you do. By now, you ought to be aware of the solution. You may wish to end your relationship because your spouse has been mistreating you or because you've fallen in love with someone else. Another illustration is getting married at a young age. You haven't explored the possibilities in this situation to identify your genuine soul match. Don't hold back and deprive yourself of happiness. Even though breaking up with someone you've been dating can be unpleasant, you'll eventually start to forget about them over the next months.

Moving on can take years for some people. This is so because when people are dating, they frequently compare their partners to their ex. The worst thing you could possibly do is this. Instead, concentrate on the person's strengths. Additionally, keep an eye out for any red flags. Moving on too quickly is harmful, and if you're still thinking about your ex, you won't be able to appreciate your new relationship.

CHAPTER 1
ENDING A RELATIONSHIP

Prior to ending a relationship, you must consider how to break the news to your partner. They at least deserve that much. Put your thoughts and the reasons you desire to move on in writing. When you chat to them, be sure to express your love and let them know you will miss them. Shouting or arguing is the worst way to end a relationship. But keep in mind that you still need to be firm. If not, they might bully you and refuse to accept the separation. You'll need to learn how to stand your ground if your partner is manipulative, because the situation could worsen if you don’t.

TIPS

Here are some suggestions for breaking up with someone:

Meet them in person at a coffee, restaurant, or shopping mall. If they decide to erupt, this will make the environment secure.

Tell them how much you care about them and how moving on would be painful to not only them, but to you also. It's a good idea to express your emotions.

When speaking to your partner, make eye contact and maintain a firm tone to convey your sincerity.

Before addressing the issues in the relationship, tell them what you liked most about it. By doing this, you not only draw attention to their problematic habits but also to their positive traits.

Discuss whether you want to be friends or stay apart with them. You must reach a conclusion. Setting boundaries for one another without allowing anyone else to interfere with your lives is what is meant by this.

Talk about specifics when you're around friends and relatives. Pick whether to inform the other party(ies) of the breakup.

When outlining your reasons for the breakup, speak carefully and reassuringly.

You want to be sure that your partner understands everything.

Keep your cool if they try to create a scene. However, if the situation worsens, let them know that you must leave. Inform them that you don't want to fight or create a scene. Hopefully they'll understand and stop being upset before you go.

These are some of the best methods for ending a relationship. There is a minor probability that things may blow up in your face or turn into an argument because you will be in a crowded area. Though it would be exceedingly embarrassing for the other person you are breaking up with, never bring a friend or family member with you.

CHAPTER 2
A BAD RELATIONSHIP

We are all aware that certain people are persuasive, cunning, and promising in certain ways. Breaking up with someone who behaves in this manner won't be simple.

Most likely, they'll come up to you and assure you that everything will return to normal. They might even come off as sincere, with their undesirable habits disappearing. Keep in mind that everything they are doing is just an act, and that most people won't change until they truly care about you. It's a good indication that they are not interested in changing if they conduct in the same manner around their friends while simply putting on a front for you.

Some breakups are so painful for the other person that they believe they are unable to move on with their lives. They are a mess as their emotions start to flood in. They experience a sense of loss without you in their life. You should take the situation seriously when your ex is like this. Take your ex seriously if they bring up suicide. As you call the police, continue your text conversation with them. These people are delicate when it comes to relationships. If they're lying, your ex will soon discover the repercussions, and won't do this again. When the police are contacted, they will take your ex to the closest psychiatric institution, which also serves as a suicide prevention facility. The knowledge that your ex is secure will make you pleased. They will bring the person to these locations and place them in a room with just a bed. There aren't any substantial items in the room that they may use to commit suicide. There will be 24/7 surveillance of the room. They may keep the person there for a day or maybe a week. If they need to talk to someone, there will be a counselling session for them.

Be careful of your ex, if such person is manipulative in nature, as they might want to harm you. Make sure you alert the authorities if they intend to use blackmail in an illegal manner. The best course of action is to absolutely avoid these folks because they are, at best, ruthless. This entails to finding another job in a different location, phone number, and possibly even your school. Obviously, if there is no way to contact you, they cannot blackmail you. Tell your family members to ignore any calls from your ex.

Here are some relationship advice to help you from bad relationships.

MANIPULATION

Did you realize that the main factor keeping men and women together is manipulation? For instance, if you tell your lady that you want to break up with her due to her poor behaviors, she will use guilt to her advantage to control you. She suddenly adopts a dejected expression as her cheeks begins to flow with tears. She claims she will kill herself without you, and you worry that she'll do something stupid, like kill herself. Instead, get assistance for her immediately and advance gently. Take some time to get away from her without telling her openly that you are moving on.

AGGRESSION

You can avoid getting into an abusive relationship by learning to recognize aggressive behaviors in men. Men that are aggressive often grasp your arm, urge you to do things you don't want to do, or even compel you to participate in something you don't want to. You could assume that this is merely a characteristic of his personality, but it's not.

LOW SELF ESTEEM

Low self esteem can result from being in a relationship that is physically or mentally abusive. You no longer seem to be the jovial, upbeat person you once were; instead, you appear to be walking around with your shoulders hunched. Your old hobbies are no longer enjoyable, and this poor self-esteem will eventually cause sadness.

BLACKMAIL

Blackmail frequently results in low self-esteem. She may have captured some explicit photos of you in your underwear when you and your ex were together. She threatens to send these to every girl you know if you leave her. Even if they are unable to be with you, someone who truly loved you would be concerned about your feelings.

PHYSICAL ABUSE

Men and women are both capable of abusing one another physically. It doesn't apply only to guys. In reality, a lot of women have been known to physically abuse their partner. Physical abuse is severe, so if it's happening to you, get away. It is crucial to get in touch with your local police enforcement if you have bruises from the abuse. Don't allow them to treat you this way. There are many excellent people out there who will treat you with the respect and decency you merit.

MENTAL ABUSE

No fun at all to be subjected to mental abuse. Name-calling, making fun of, and even being humiliated in front of others frequently mark the beginning of mental abuse. Say your partner enjoys disparaging you in front of his friends. He wants to come out as strong and in charge. Actually, this guy doesn't care about your feelings, and the mental torture will just become worse. While you still have time, leave.

CHAPTER 3

HOW TO EASILY END A RELATIONSHIP

Nowadays, breaking up is difficult, unless you stick to a phone conversation or text. Instead, you should take care of everything in person. Never pass the message to a friend, and never, never, never write about it. These types breakups are among the worst. To avoid them refusing to meet with you, make sure to schedule a date to meet your partner while keeping them in the dark about your breakup.

Tips on what not to do after splitting up are provided below:

- Never try to end a relationship via text or letter.
- Before you schedule a date, don't tell your spouse that you're thinking about breaking up.
- Never use an aggressive tone or insults when breaking up.
- Never try to end a relationship via text message, phone call or letter.
- Never break up with a partner after telling your friends first, let them be the first to know. Do not end a relationship in front of people well known to both of you.
- Never announce it around that your relationship is ending.

These are unquestionably the worst methods to end a relationship, thus it is advisable to be respectful of that individual if you wish to remain friends. This will offer you an opportunity to maintain a positive friendship with them and avoid situations that can cause stress. It's true that ending a relationship is unpleasant at best. When you learn that the girl or man of your dreams is leaving you, feelings that you have never experienced before frequently come up and can easily explode. You'll frequently feel abandoned, depressed, and lost.

Be aware that not everyone can remain friends after a breakup. You should accept it if your partner doesn't want to be friends after you break up with them. They might find the sorrow of knowing they can't be with you too much to bear. There is a possibility that it will improve with time. There is a good potential that you might return when she begins to appreciate life without you by spending more time with her friends, beginning to work on her education, and having fun. Now, we mean return as a friend rather than a husband/wife or a boyfriend/girlfriend.

What if your former partner from six months ago gets in touch with you on twitter? Please don't assume he wants to rekindle your relationship. Just remember that he still cares about you and merely wants to know how you are doing. You have no idea if he is dating, lives abroad, or just has a busy schedule right now. Although changes can be made rapidly, occasionally people choose to remain in their current positions. Make sure to have an open mind and avoid making hasty judgments.

CHAPTER 4
COUNSELLING AND GUIDANCE

Hundreds of relationships end each day for the wrong reasons. For instance, you might be dating a beautiful guy who loves you dearly but doesn't express it verbally. You've seen that he behaves in this manner towards everyone, even family members. He still doesn't talk much, despite the fact that you two have been dating for five months. However, because he is deeply in love with you, this guy is preparing to purpose to you. Unconditional love is the act of accepting someone as they are. You should think twice before you end things if he treats you nicely and has a kind heart.

Let's first discuss the value of counseling. You can express your disappointments or frustrations without disputes by going to a relationship therapist once a week. This is a safe approach to conduct civil conversations on anything. The counselor's job is to keep track of your development and make sure that the session doesn't end in conflicts, which frequently occurs with couples. Most of the time, a person will hold back their emotions out of fear of what the other person—in this case, the therapist—might think.

What about ending a relationship to pursue a new love? Although it has been tried by many, this is the worst concept. Almost everything around the house is done by your wife, a stressed out stay-at-home mother. She is incredibly friendly and nice. She transforms into someone else by the time you go back home. She is yelling at you and demanding that you make more contribution. It's her way of asking for assistance with the kids. She is upset because she was unable to take care of a couple of her needs today. You've recently spoken with her former coworker's pals. Her friend is really intelligent and gorgeous. You've always been curious about how things might go, so you're considering breaking up with your fiancée. Have you ever considered that your fiancée may have developed stress when she began looking after the kids at home? The new girl you like might experience the same thing, particularly if a serious connection develops.

CHAPTER 5
SOLUTIONS

Even though you were the one to start the breakup, you could find it very challenging to move on. It is also common to feel regret after ending a relationship, and you might need to restrain yourself from texting or calling your ex. Let's assume that their terrible behaviors caused your breakup. Your partner frequently arrives late, smokes, and swears at your family. You attempted to make him change because you believed he was capable of doing so. Unfortunately, he never will.

All of those things, however, cannot compensate for the way he treats your family. You must put an end to it and continue. If you don't, your family can start to ignore you and gradually distance themselves from you.

Before continuing, we suggest a few tried-and-true relationship solutions, which are given below. This could be your chance to save the relationship, so read carefully.

TALK

You must have "the conversation" before continuing. They'll understand how significant this is for you if you let them know where you're going with this. You can express your disappointment and frustrations in a relationship through talking. Inform them of the behaviors you don't like and offer suggestions for improvement.

PROMISES

Why not make promises to one another if you two are aware that your relationship is unhealthy? For instance, if your lover insults you by calling you names out of rage, have him swear not to do so again. He will asks and stop making fun of him in front of his buddies. A boundary between both of you is very helpful.

LOVE

Do you believe that your current partner is making you question your love for them? If this is the case, you might want to try rekindling the magic and see what you can do to restore it to how it was when the two of you met. Why not visit a restaurant that the two of you used to go to relive old memories? Make it unique. If you'd like, light candles or bring flowers. This will undoubtedly rekindle the flames!

You cannot move within a short period of time. Even if the breakup was your idea, it might take months or even years to get over a significant other you love very much.You'll want to run away if you're stuck in a relationship you're unhappy with. You've also started attending church with your spouse and tried counseling together. Nothing you did changed anything. You must stop now because of this. It's a dead end if you've tried everything and there are no more possibilities. Keep in mind that the world is not ending. You'll probably run into a new person.

You must force yourself to engage in new things if you want to advance. Take your friends out more often. When you're feeling down, especially if you can't stop thinking about your ex, a girls' night out is always a terrific way to lift your spirits.

Why not devote a couple more hours to your job? You can make some extra cash while distracting yourself from your ex. However, if he or she works where you do, you should probably look for another job .

The hardest time of day is at night. When you reflect on old experiences, your heart and mind will feel confused. You could then feel the desire to give them a call or send a text. Pick up a nice book instead of crying and letting your feelings overwhelm you. You can stop caring about the other person and put your attention on your own needs by reading every night.

It Is a good to ask for assistance from others if you are still having problems moving on. You'll be able to pinpoint what bothers you the most by using your communication skills. You can choose to receive counseling if you feel uncomfortable or if you have no friends with whom to discuss things. Your counselor is there to listen to your feelings and perhaps to offer suggestions for action. Additionally, they'll keep tabs on your development and let you know if they notice any encouraging developments. Keep a journal with you at all times while you are getting counseling. You won't be as fixated on your ex as you once were over time.

CHAPTER 6
RESPONDING TO GOOD AND BAD ADVICE

You must be self-assured and conscious of your surroundings in order to respond to both the good and the advice on ending a relationship. When deciding to leave a relationship, communication is another important consideration. Make sure to pay attention to these three areas. Otherwise, it might not work out so well when people advice you to stay in a bad relationship. When people realize that a relationship is no longer beneficial to their emotional and physical wellbeing, both men and women mostly end the relationship.

Here are some suggestions for when you feel it's time to exit a relationship.

CONFIDENCE

It's crucial to have faith in your ability to move forward. At this time, you may feel as though you are incapable of loving someone else, but this is untrue. You'll gradually start to feel better as time passes, making way for brand-new connections to arise. Do not wallow in your room; instead, leave the house. Join community activities like volunteering if you want to. This is a fantastic technique to relax and let your guard down among others. There are numerous volunteer activities available, including gardening, garbage collection, joining a health center, and assisting helpless kids. You'll be sure that you'll recover quickly if you have confidence. All you need to do is believe in yourself.

CONSCIOUSNESS

Your first step toward healing is becoming conscious of your emotions. It's acceptable to cry occasionally. You might continue to feel angry or depressed if you don't express your emotions. You won't be able to move on and take charge of your life because of it. Music can frequently be a great aid if you struggle to be conscious of your emotions. Play music with lyrics that convey strong emotions. The same feelings will start to come over you as well.

INTERACT

You will feel better and be able to get through this condition if you are able to communicate with other people. You are letting out any feelings you may have through interacting with people. You can discuss the situation with your friends and relatives. They will either provide you advice or simply act as a listening ear. Usually, when someone acknowledges us in life, a gate will open. The route that passes by this gate leads to tranquility, joy, and harmony.

CHAPTER 7
BENEFITS

Moving is probably not a good option if you are unsure about your decision to do so. You must decide whether the relationship has hope and is worthwhile of being saved. There are many advantages to being satisfied in a relationship, and by leaving, you miss out on these advantages. Here are some suggestions for getting through everything and identifying the cause of all your problems. Although the person you are with could be incredibly excellent for you, you first need assistance. Although change is always conceivable, it cannot be effected by force. The most effective method for resolving communication issues and assisting your significant other in forming healthy habits is to offer positive encouragement for change.

To find a solution, it's crucial to discuss any issues in your relationship with your partner. Consider leaving if they appear unprepared for any adjustments or hesitating. Give them a chance if they decide to change. They might revert to their previous behavior in the future, at which point it will be time to end the relationship. You ought to be with someone who values you highly enough to make a change in their behavior.

Making sacrifices is what love is all about.

Go over anything that the two of you are having issues with. It might not be due to a significant issue. Divorce frequently occurs as a result of numerous minor issues that compound over time. You two can be enraged with one another and possibly taking revenge. It is clear that this is not good for the relationship. Tell your spouse what is bothering you so that you may begin to make improvements.

When talking about issues, don't accuse them or yell at them. After complimenting them on anything they accomplished today, move on to the next topic. You might even make your spouse feel guilty if you express your feelings to your spouse after they do anything specific. Making them feel guilty is not the intended outcome, but it might work. Your partner will understand that you are sensitive and may even apologize as they look for solutions to the issue. Keep in mind that how you present the topic, not what you say, matters.

CHAPTER 8
MOVING ON

You can become a stronger person in the future by moving on without him. Even though moving on could be one of the hardest things you ever do, it will be for the best. You wouldn't want to spend time with someone who is aggressive, selfish, and unconcerned about your feelings.

The benefit of moving on is that you won't have to let him pull your emotions down with him. You will become less confident in yourself if you are among people who treat you poorly. As you move on, surround yourself with encouraging individuals. To lift your spirits, you can go out with a few of your friends. They can help you out because I'm sure they've experienced similar things. Staying with your ex-partner could make you depressed.

For instance, if your lover has already cheated on you three times in the relationship, this will make you feel depressed. You may even believe that anything is wrong with you. Don't I look good enough for him? You aren't the cause of the issue. Some men are merely not prepared to settle down and modify their behaviors. This is especially true if they are younger.

This does not imply that you should go out and date other men. Instead, pay attention to yourself. How can you improve your personality and form healthy habits? You can meet others who share your interests by doing things like attending to school, showing up for work, and even participating in some activities. It's a good idea to just meet women, but it's also okay if you make a few male buddies along the road. Create a few friendships rather than go on dates. In the future, you might be prepared to date once more, and who knows, the guy you like might even be waiting for this moment.

CONCLUSION

There are many good reasons for moving forward without him. He can be preventing you from meeting a guy who would be excellent for you or from doing things in life that you'd like to do. Whether you are a young woman or an elderly woman, it doesn't matter. There is still a lot of life left for us to explore. In just a few months, a lot can happen.

Always keep in mind that occasionally we move on for a cause. It will get better, even if you don't think you could break up with your lover. The heart always heals with time. After a few years, you might miss him, but you'll meet someone else. You will then understand there are nice men out there when you find someone else who is better for you and treats you well. Although they are hard to come by, if you start spending time with people who have positive habits, you won't be setting yourself up for failure. Here are a few reasons for leaving him behind.

1. Be in charge of your life's objectives.
2. Improve your family relationships and create stronger ones.
3. Start praying to God for guidance.
4. Not experiencing harassment or abuse.

5. Cease being influenced and manipulated.

6. To live a life filled with new and better experiences.

7. Enjoy life to the fullest without letting him hold you back.

8. Pay attention to your physical and mental health.

9. Freedom from a person who doesn't genuinely love you

10. Leave a man who doesn't respect you.

11. Cherish your friendships more
12. Create a secure space for yourself.

13. Get to know who you are.
14. Put your education first.

15. Have the ability to focus on your career.
16. Surround yourself with optimistic individuals

17. Establish a solid bond with yourself (spiritual)

18. Recognize and express your emotions.

19. Get the chance to meet other good-looking men.

www.ingramcontent.com/pod-product-compliance
Lightning Source LLC
LaVergne TN
LVHW050348160826
845677LV00014B/3863

* 9 7 9 8 8 4 8 7 1 8 2 7 0 *